Original title:

The Heart's Compass

Copyright © 2024 Swan Charm

All rights reserved.

Author: Liina Liblikas

ISBN HARDBACK: 978-9916-89-199-5

ISBN PAPERBACK: 978-9916-89-200-8

ISBN EBOOK: 978-9916-89-201-5

The Windward Way of Love

In morning light the whispers sway,
Where tender hearts in silence play.
With dreams that dance on breezes bright,
They find their way through day and night.

Each glance a spark, a gentle fire,
As souls entwine, they rise higher.
With laughter's sound and soft embrace,
They carve their path, to love's sweet grace.

Along the shore where waves collide,
They walk as one, with hearts as guide.
In every storm, in every sigh,
The windward way, they learn to fly.

Through seasons change, their spirits blend,
With every twist, their love won't end.
In stillness found and tempests braved,
The windward way, forever paved.

So let the whispers fill the air,
In each caress, in every care.
The journey long, yet ever new,
The windward way, their love so true.

Wayfaring Through Sentiment

On a road paved with whispers,
Dreams flutter like leaves.
Beneath the arch of silence,
Hope dances and weaves.

Each step whispers stories,
Echoing fears long held.
With every breath we take,
Our truths are slowly spelled.

In the warmth of soft sunlight,
Heartbeats gently collide.
A symphony of feelings,
Together we confide.

Through valleys rich with yearning,
And mountains draped in doubt,
We gather our lost pieces,
In trust, we find the route.

But through the weeping twilight,
New paths begin to show.
With every footfall taken,
The heart learns how to grow.

A Path Through Shadows

In the hush of twilight's glow,
Shadows stretch and lend their grace.
Each corner turned, whispers flow,
Guiding the silent chase.

Flickering lights in the distance,
A promise of what may come.
Through the mist of existence,
We march, though we feel numb.

Lost in echoes of the night,
The moon drapes us in silver.
With every step, we take flight,
Seeking where futures deliver.

Yet whispers of doubt may cling,
As threads of darkness entwine.
But hope is a fragile zing,
That glimmers, ever divine.

So onward through darkened lanes,
With hearts made of stardust bright.
For even through countless pains,
We emerge into the light.

Riddles of the Heart

Tangled thoughts in twilight's grasp,
Heartbeats dance, a soft embrace.
In silence, riddles form and clasp,
Within each hidden trace.

What lies beneath the surface,
In the chambers, dimly lit?
Secrets weave their subtle purpose,
In every heartbeat's wit.

Fingers touch the edges bare,
Of love, and loss combined.
Though questions linger in the air,
The answers are entwined.

A glance shared, a fleeting sigh,
Words spoken without tone.
Through every tear that we dry,
A bond is gently grown.

So let the heart be patient,
With riddles, it must play.
For in the depth of silence,
Love finds its own way.

Sails of Understandings

Upon the sea of sorrow,
We hoist our sails of dreams.
Navigating through tomorrow,
With heartfelt, whispered themes.

The winds of change may tussle,
Yet we stand firm and true.
Charting journeys through the bustle,
With every wave, anew.

At dawn, we catch the sunlight,
Painting horizons wide.
Through storms that roar with might,
We shall not be denied.

With every bond we foster,
And every truth we share,
We find that love can prosper,
In waters rich and rare.

So let us sail together,
To lands yet uncharted, bold.
For in the heart's endeavor,
Lies treasure worth more than gold.

My Heart's Atlas

In the quiet folds of night,
Where dreams and shadows blend tight,
I trace the paths of old desires,
With every heartbeat, my soul inspires.

Through valleys deep and hills of gold,
Memories whisper, tales unfold.
Each step a longing, a hope, a quest,
In this cartography, I find my rest.

The stars above map my fears,
Each twinkle a reflection of tears.
But in the darkness, light does glow,
Guiding me where love can grow.

With every map, each line I draw,
I find the beauty in every flaw.
Though roads may twist and sometimes bend,
In my heart's atlas, love has no end.

Navigating through the years,
Collecting moments, joys, and fears.
This journey shapes who I have been,
A compass to the love within.

The Intersection of Souls

In the space where silence hums,
Two hearts converge, the magic comes.
A glance that speaks, a touch that yearns,
In this moment, the universe turns.

Paths cross like lines on a map,
In this fervent, fateful lap.
What started as whispers in the air,
Now weaves a tapestry rare.

Like rivers flowing, we entwine,
Every challenge, our love will shine.
A journey shared, we build anew,
An intersection of me and you.

Laughter echoes through the night,
Turning darkness into light.
In each heartbeat, a story told,
In this crossing, our souls unfold.

Together we navigate the space,
Finding comfort in each embrace.
In this dance of fate's design,
Your soul's sweet melody with mine.

Maps of the Melancholy

In the atlas of my heavy heart,
Lies a world built on dreams apart.
Each page a tear, each line a sigh,
Through sorrow's shadows, I learn to fly.

Silent whispers in the dark,
Echoes of joy that leave a mark.
Mapping the echoes of what once was,
Finding solace in nature's pause.

The rain falls soft, a gentle guide,
Painting memories we cannot hide.
As I wander through my past's embrace,
I search for light, a hint of grace.

With ink of tears, I sketch my pain,
In every drop, a melancholic strain.
Yet within the sorrow's tender hold,
Lie the stories that need to be told.

These maps I chart lead me to peace,
As I find in heartache, a quiet release.
In melancholy's depth, I'll rise anew,
With every journey, I'll find what's true.

Constant North of Connection

Under skies of endless blue,
We seek the threads that link me and you.
A compass forged in hearts of gold,
A guiding light, our stories unfold.

Through storms and trials, we find our way,
In the wilderness, love will stay.
Each moment shared, a beacon bright,
In darkness, you are my light.

The map we draw is ever wide,
With each path taken, love as our guide.
Through life's maze, we are never lost,
Together we bear every cost.

With every heartbeat, we redefine,
The constant north, your hand in mine.
In this connection, we will thrive,
With love as our anchor, we are alive.

As seasons change and time moves on,
Our bond remains, forever strong.
A journey without an end in sight,
In connection, we find our light.

Symbols in the Sky

Clouds drift by like thoughts,
Shapes that tell a tale,
Whispers of the cosmos,
Secrets in the veil.

Stars sparkle with a purpose,
Guiding dreams afloat,
Constellations weave their stories,
In the night, they wrote.

Moonlight bathes the silence,
Casting shadows bright,
Echoes of lost lovers,
Dance in silver light.

Rain paints down like memories,
Each drop a sweet refrain,
Nature's rhythm pulses,
In joy and in pain.

Winds carry the wishes,
To places far and wide,
With every breath of stardust,
Hope and dreams collide.

Fables of Affection

In gardens blooming bright,
Love finds its gentle way,
Petals whisper soft secrets,
On a sunlit day.

Hands held in silence,
Comfort in the night,
Hearts beat like a drum,
In a tender light.

Stories shared in laughter,
Moments pure and rare,
Each glance a warm embrace,
A connection we share.

Through storms and the struggles,
Our bonds only grow,
In the fables of affection,
Love's light always glows.

As seasons keep on changing,
We stand side by side,
In the tale of our lives,
Endless love is our guide.

Echoing Footsteps

Footsteps on the pavement,
Memories of the past,
Each echo tells a story,
Of shadows that we cast.

In the park, laughter lingers,
Children play and run,
Their joy like the sun's rays,
Chasing the day's fun.

Leaves crunch beneath our weight,
As autumn's breath draws near,
With every step we carry,
Both laughter and a tear.

Paths cross and intertwine,
In a dance so divine,
With every echo passing,
Hearts within us align.

The journey, ever winding,
Leads us to the light,
In the echoes of our footsteps,
We find love's pure sight.

The Way Home

The road stretches ahead,
Beneath the twilight sky,
With every step I take,
I feel my spirit fly.

Stars begin to twinkle,
Guiding lost souls like me,
Through valleys and the hills,
To where I long to be.

Whispers in the wind call,
Tales of those who roam,
Through trials and the laughter,
I see my way back home.

With shadows in my footprints,
And the moon as my guide,
Courage fills my heart now,
As love will not divide.

The journey bears its riches,
In the moments we share,
The way home brings us closer,
With every breath of air.

Mapping Intimacy

In quiet whispers, secrets bloom,
Hearts entwined within the room.
Each glance a map, each touch a line,
Navigating love, so pure, divine.

We chart our course through tangled dreams,
Where laughter flows and sunlight streams.
With every heartbeat, paths unfold,
In intimacy, our stories told.

Fingers tracing unspoken thoughts,
In the spaces, warmth is sought.
Every silence speaks in tone,
In shared breaths, we are not alone.

The Longitude of Longing

Across the sea of dreams we sail,
Longing whispers through the veil.
With every wave, our hearts align,
In the longitude where love will shine.

Stars above, a guiding light,
Charting courses through the night.
With hope as wind, we glide and drift,
In this journey, love's our gift.

Every moment brings us near,
In longing's ache, we persevere.
Together in this vast expanse,
We find our way through chance and chance.

Footprints in the Sand of Time

On golden shores, our footprints lay,
In shifting sands, they fade away.
Each step a tale, a moment shared,
In time's embrace, we both have dared.

The ocean's breath, it calls our names,
In whispered tides, love softly claims.
As waves retreat and shadows grow,
Our footprints mark the paths we know.

Through storms and sun, through joy and pain,
Our memories dance like gentle rain.
Each grain of sand, a story fine,
In the vastness, our hearts entwine.

The Radiance of Connection

In the stillness, our spirits meet,
Where silence wraps us in its heat.
A spark ignites, a warm embrace,
In connection's glow, we find our place.

Like constellations in the sky,
Each twinkle speaks, and soars high.
Bound by threads of light that shine,
In the glow of love, we intertwine.

With every laughter, every tear,
The radiance brightens, drawing near.
In every heartbeat, we reflect,
In this connection, we are blessed.

The Rhythm of Belonging

In the heart's quiet space, we find,
A melody that gently binds.
Voices weave, in sweet embrace,
Creating warmth in every trace.

Through laughter shared, and tears that fall,
In the midst of chaos, we stand tall.
United by a common song,
Together, where we all belong.

Moments pass like leaves in fall,
Yet in this rhythm, we hear the call.
The pulse of life, a steady beat,
In every bond, a joy complete.

Whispers echo in the night,
Instead of shadows, we find light.
Hands held tightly, spirits soar,
In the dance of trust, we seek for more.

Through every trial, every change,
In the tapestry, we rearrange.
The rhythm soft, yet bold and strong,
In belonging's arms, we all belong.

Footprints in the Sand

Upon the shore, where waters kiss,
Footprints linger in ocean's bliss.
Each step a story, each grain a sigh,
Memories woven, as the tide goes by.

The sun dips low, a golden hue,
Casting shadows of me and you.
In the shifting sands, we roam free,
Tracing our love in harmony.

Waves will wash and winds will blow,
Yet the mark remains in ebb and flow.
In the quiet moments, here we stand,
Together, leaving footprints in the sand.

As dusk embraces the fading light,
Our hearts dance in the coming night.
With every wave, we're drawn anew,
To the rhythm of dreams, just us two.

Gone with the tide but forever near,
In every shell, we hold what's dear.
Footprints fade, but love's command,
Lives on forever, hand in hand.

A Trail of Tenderness

In the garden of hearts where kindness grows,
A trail of tenderness gently flows.
Each whispered word, a petal's grace,
Softly nurtured in love's embrace.

With every gesture, no matter how small,
A spark ignites, illuminating all.
The warmth of laughter, the comfort of tears,
A bond that strengthens through all the years.

Beneath the stars, where dreams unite,
We wander together, guided by light.
In shared silence, understanding blooms,
Creating harmony in the quiet rooms.

Through storms we walk, hand in hand,
Together we rise, together we stand.
In the tapestry woven from heart to heart,
Each thread a promise, never to part.

A trail of tenderness, soft and true,
A journey of love, just me and you.
In every moment, let our hearts blend,
Creating a path that will never end.

Lost and Found in Emotion

In the labyrinth of feelings deep,
Where shadows stir and secrets sleep.
We lose ourselves, yet seek to find,
The echoes of what's in our mind.

Tears may fall like summer rain,
Washing away the weight of pain.
In the chaos, we learn to feel,
The raw truth that love can heal.

Each heartbeat sings a silent song,
A melody where we belong.
Entwined in dreams, we're often tossed,
Yet in love's arms, we're never lost.

From joy to sorrow, we'll always roam,
In every heartbeat that feels like home.
Through trials faced and battles won,
We rise again, two souls as one.

In the dance of life, we ebb and flow,
Together we thrive, together we grow.
In the depths of emotion, side by side,
We find our way, with love as our guide.

A Voyage through Vulnerability

In the quiet of the night, I sail,
Through whispers of doubt, I start to unveil.
Each wave a challenge, each storm a test,
Yet in my heart, I seek the rest.

With every tear, the sail unfurls,
Guiding me gently through shifting worlds.
Embracing the depths, where shadows play,
I find my strength in the light of day.

The stars above, like dreams in flight,
Illuminate paths cloaked in night.
In the depths of fear, I learn to trust,
For the journey is precious, and so is my lust.

Each scar a story, each bruise a part,
Of a map that leads to a willing heart.
With sails wide open, I greet the tide,
In vulnerability's arms, I now confide.

With courage as my compass, I tread anew,
A voyage of self, where the heart breaks through.
In the stillness, I find my way,
A dance with the waves, come what may.

The Compass of Yearning

In the depths of night, a flicker of light,
Guides me through shadows, takes flight.
With every pulse, my heartbeats speak,
Whispering truths, the brave and the weak.

Yearning for moments, both near and far,
I follow the whispers, my own North Star.
Each dream a compass, a map in my mind,
Leading me forward, the lost I will find.

Across open waters, I drift and I glide,
Searching for shores where my hopes can reside.
With every step, a promise of more,
In the compass of yearning, I explore the shore.

Echoes of longing awaken my soul,
Each heartbeat a story, making me whole.
In the depths of desire, I learn to believe,
That the journey itself is the gift we receive.

Through valleys of silence, I rise and I roam,
With yearning as a guide, I create my home.
In the tapestry woven from dreams that I chase,
The compass of yearning keeps me in grace.

Heartbeats in Harmony

In the rhythm of life where dreams align,
Heartbeats echo, softly entwine.
With every pulse, a song takes flight,
Melodies dancing in the quiet night.

Silent whispers, tender and true,
In the space between, I reach out to you.
Together we move, like waves on the sea,
In heartbeats of harmony, just you and me.

Through trials and triumphs, we find our way,
In the cadence of moments, we choose to stay.
Each heartbeat a promise, a bond unbroken,
In the language of love, our hearts have spoken.

Under the stars, our symphony plays,
Crafting a future from the threads of our days.
With hands held tightly, we face the unknown,
In the heartbeat of harmony, we've truly grown.

As seasons shift and days turn to years,
In rhythms of laughter and sometimes of tears,
We find our peace in the softest refrain,
In heartbeats of harmony, love will remain.

The Path of Perseverance

Through winding roads where shadows lie,
I walk with purpose, head held high.
Each step a promise, each breath a chance,
On the path of perseverance, I advance.

The weight of doubt may pull me low,
Yet in the struggle, my spirit will grow.
With grit like steel and heart of fire,
I forge ahead, fueled by desire.

Mountains may rise, and rivers may bend,
But I'll carry on, for I will not end.
Each stumble a lesson, each fall a start,
On this journey, I gather my heart.

In the echoes of failure, I find my voice,
With hope as my anchor, I make my choice.
Through storms that rage and winds that wail,
On the path of perseverance, I shall prevail.

With every dawn, a new day to claim,
I rise with resilience, igniting the flame.
In the tapestry woven by trials and tears,
The path of perseverance conquers fears.

Labyrinth of Longing

In shadows deep, the whispers call,
A heartbeat lost within the thrall.
Each turn I take, a question blooms,
A yearning voice amid the gloom.

Footsteps trace forgotten dreams,
Along the path where hope still gleams.
Through tangled vines of want and need,
In this maze, my heart shall plead.

Twilight paints the walls in gold,
A story of the brave, the bold.
With every sigh, the echoes blend,
In labyrinths, my soul to mend.

The night reveals what day obscured,
In longing's grasp, I find the cured.
Each twist and turn, a lesson learned,
In passionate fires, my heart has burned.

And as I wander, hoping free,
The maze will gift its mystery.
For in this journey, I will find,
The treasure sought, my heart aligned.

The Compass Rose of Yearning

Upon the sea of dreams I sail,
With stars above, I chart my trail.
The compass points to what I seek,
A whispered love, a voice so meek.

Every wave speaks truths untold,
In longing's light, my heart grows bold.
Through stormy nights and calmest days,
Your light will guide through love's sweet maze.

The winds of fate, they shift and tease,
In silent vows, my spirit's ease.
I follow where your shadows lead,
In every heartbeat, love's decree.

With every star that fills the sky,
I chase the dreams that never die.
For in this quest, I find my home,
No longer lost, no need to roam.

The compass rose, it steers me true,
Through every longing, leading you.
Together on this vast expanse,
We'll dance through time, in love's sweet trance.

Celestial Navigations

Underneath the velvet night,
I seek your gaze, your guiding light.
The universe, a canvas wide,
In cosmic dreams, our hearts reside.

Galaxies whisper tales of old,
In constellations, love unfolds.
Each star a wish that's yet to bloom,
In celestial paths, dispelling gloom.

With every comet's fleeting flight,
I feel your presence in the night.
In astral winds, our spirits soar,
Through endless skies, forevermore.

Navigating through the dark,
Your love, my beacon, sparks the arc.
Together, we will chase the dawn,
In stellar dreams, our hearts reborn.

So let the universe conspire,
To weave our fate in love's sweet fire.
Through cosmic dances, we will find,
Eternal bonds that fate designed.

Lanterns in the Dark

In shadows where the secrets lie,
The lanterns flicker, softly nigh.
They speak of hope, of tales untold,
In gentle light, our fears unfold.

Each flame a wish, a flickering dream,
A guiding spark, a silver beam.
Through darkest nights, we hold them high,
In every heartbeat, our spirits fly.

They cast a glow on hidden paths,
Illuminating love's sweet laughs.
Together, we shall face the night,
With hearts aglow, in shared delight.

The journey winds through every fear,
But with your hand, I draw you near.
In lanterns' glow, our courage grows,
Through every trial, true love shows.

So let us roam where shadows play,
With lanterns bright, we'll find our way.
For in the dark, we learn to see,
The light of love, forever free.

Journeys Between Us

Two paths converge, where dreams reside,
Hearts entwined, side by side.
Beyond the hills, the sun will rise,
With every step, our spirits fly.

Moments shared, a tapestry spun,
Laughter and tears, always one.
In silent nights, we find our way,
Through whispers soft, love leads the day.

Each mile walked, a story told,
In warmth of touch, and hands to hold.
The stars above, our guiding light,
Together strong, we face the night.

In valleys deep, or mountains high,
With open hearts, we learn to fly.
Through storms and calm, our bond stays true,
Every journey starts with me and you.

At twilight's kiss, our shadows blend,
In every path, we find the end.
The road ahead, forever bright,
Embracing all, through day and night.

Coordinates of Compassion

In the map of hearts, we chart our course,
With kindness as our central source.
Every gesture, a point in time,
Together we rise, in love's soft rhyme.

Guiding hands, we navigate,
Through trials shared, we cultivate.
In gentle words, our compass lies,
As empathy blooms, our spirits rise.

Through winding roads, we learn to care,
In every gaze, a bond we share.
Each step we take, a vow so clear,
With open hearts, we conquer fear.

In the silent spaces, love will guide,
With trust as shelter, we won't subside.
Coordinates drawn, two souls aligned,
In this vast world, true kin we find.

As the years turn, we'll journey on,
Through night and day, our hearts a song.
Connected forever, in each embrace,
With coordinates of care, we find our place.

The Guide to Togetherness

In the forest lush, we wander near,
Trust our hearts, as we draw near.
Each step we take, a promise made,
In the dance of love, we won't fade.

Through tangled vines, our hands held tight,
In shadows cast, we find the light.
With every laugh, the journey's sweet,
Together we bloom, love's purest feat.

In every challenge, we stand as one,
With voices raised, our song begun.
Navigating dreams, both bold and bright,
In this journey, together, we write.

Through every storm, our spirits soar,
In the silence, we yearn for more.
As the stars align, we set our sights,
On the horizon, where hope ignites.

With hearts as guides, we find our pace,
In the rhythm of love, our sacred space.
Through every season, hand in hand,
The guide to togetherness, a promised land.

The Trails of Desire

By amber light, our footsteps trace,
In whispered dreams, we find our place.
Each trail we walk, ignites the fire,
With hearts ablaze, we chase desire.

Through emerald woods, we feel the pull,
In every glance, the heart is full.
With passion's spark, the world expands,
Together painting, with gentle hands.

On sun-kissed hills, our laughter rings,
In playful moments, love takes wings.
In every sigh, and every glance,
The trails of desire lead to chance.

As twilight falls, our shadows meld,
In the night sky, our fate is held.
With every heartbeat, we're intertwined,
In the depth of love, our souls aligned.

Through all our journeys, side by side,
With open hearts, and arms spread wide.
In every trail, the truth inspires,
In the depths of us, the trails of desire.

Echoes of Affection

In shadows soft, love whispers low,
A gentle breeze, where sweet dreams flow.
Hearts entwined in silent grace,
Echoes of warmth, in time and space.

Each heartbeat sings a tender tune,
Under the watch of a silver moon.
Fingers trace the lines of fate,
In every moment, hearts await.

Through laughter shared and sorrows too,
A bond that deepens, tried and true.
In the quiet, love's glow ignites,
Warmth and comfort in long, cold nights.

From whispers soft to shouts of joy,
Each memory cherished, none can destroy.
The fates conspire to keep us near,
In echoes of love, crystal clear.

So let us dance in this embrace,
In every glance, a sacred space.
Where echoes linger and hearts compose,
A symphony of what love chose.

The Map of Longing

In corners of the heart, maps unfold,
Drawing paths of dreams, both brave and bold.
With every heartbeat, distance fades,
Longing becomes the road we pave.

Stars align in a cosmic chart,
Guiding wanderers, lost in art.
Each mile traveled, a lesson learned,
In the flames of desire, passion burned.

Through deserts dry and mountains steep,
We seek the treasures our hearts keep.
In whispers soft, hopes gently cast,
A journey woven, a spell that lasts.

Each detour leads to hidden gems,
In laughter shared, in diadems.
Unfolding stories in every place,
Love's cartography we now embrace.

So we'll wander, come what may,
In the map of longing, our hearts will stay.
Together we'll chase what life imparts,
As we navigate with open hearts.

Guiding Stars of Emotion

In twilight's glow, the stars appear,
Guiding us through the depths of fear.
Each twinkle tells of dreams we chase,
In the vastness, we find our space.

Through storms we sail, on waves of doubt,
The stars remind what love's about.
With every flicker, hope ignites,
A beacon shining through the nights.

Navigating the skies of despair,
The constellations spark our prayer.
In each cluster, memories bind,
An astral map for hearts aligned.

Through tears that fall like gentle rain,
Stars whisper softly to ease the pain.
Together we'll navigate the dark,
With guiding stars, we'll find our spark.

So let our hearts light up the night,
With love's embrace, burning bright.
For in every glow, a promise stays,
Guiding us through our endless days.

Innate Navigation

In every soul, a compass lies,
Guiding us through lows and highs.
With every step, the heart does know,
Paths of love that ebb and flow.

Through twists and turns, we make our way,
Navigating night and day.
In stillness rests a knowing spark,
A light to lead us through the dark.

With every challenge, we find our course,
Trusting instinct, a silent force.
In solitude or crowded space,
Innate navigation finds its place.

So let us journey, hand in hand,
Through shifting seas, on golden sand.
For love's direction is clear and bright,
With innate navigation, we take flight.

In the dance of life, we sway and glide,
With hearts as one, our hopes as guide.
Together we'll traverse every scene,
With innate navigation, forever keen.

Routes of Resilience

In shadows deep, we find our way,
Steps taken slow, yet we won't stray.
Through storms we walk, with heads held high,
The spirit strong, it cannot die.

Every stumble, a lesson learned,
With every fall, the fire burned.
The road is rough, yet brightly gleams,
With hope that fuels our wildest dreams.

Through trials faced, we gather strength,
A journey long, we'll go the length.
Together bound, we share the load,
Side by side, we forge the road.

Resilience grows in hearts like ours,
In darkest nights, we reach for stars.
With every step, we start anew,
The paths we take, they show us truth.

With open hearts, we rise above,
Connected still by threads of love.
Through twists and turns, we won't give in,
For every end, a new begin.

Landscapes of the Soul

In quiet fields where shadows play,
The whispers of the heart convey.
A canvas wide, with colors bright,
Each stroke reveals our inner light.

Mountains high, valleys so deep,
In every crevice, secrets keep.
The rivers flow, the winds will sing,
In landscapes vast, our spirits spring.

The skies above, they shift and change,
With every hue, the worlds exchange.
In sunsets warm, we see our dreams,
Reflections soft, like gentle streams.

Through forests thick, we walk alone,
Yet in the heart, we call it home.
Each leaf that falls tells stories old,
In nature's arms, we are consoled.

So travel deep, embrace it all,
The landscapes vast, the rise, the fall.
In every breath, let spirit soar,
A journey rich, forevermore.

The Dial of Love's Journey

In tender moments, time stands still,
Two souls entwined, a shared will.
With every heartbeat, love's embrace,
A dance of light, a sacred space.

Through seasons passed, we've weathered storms,
In every trial, love transforms.
With every laugh, with every tear,
Together strong, we persevere.

In gentle whispers, the dial turns,
With passion bright, our spirit burns.
Each twist and turn, a story told,
In love's warm grasp, we find our gold.

Through winding roads, we make our way,
With trust as guide, come what may.
In every glance, a silent vow,
With you, my love, I'm strong somehow.

So let us journey, side by side,
With open hearts, let love be our guide.
For every moment, a gift to share,
A timeless bond, beyond compare.

Where Hearts Align

In quiet spaces where silence breathes,
Two hearts converge, like autumn leaves.
With every glance, emotions spoke,
In shared smiles, the barriers broke.

On tides of time, our spirits flow,
In harmony, we ebb and glow.
With hands held tight, we cross the line,
In this sweet dance, where hearts align.

Through gentle days and starry nights,
In love's embrace, we find the lights.
With every beat, our stories blend,
In woven dreams, our journeys mend.

In laughter shared, in whispers low,
The lengths we go, it helps us grow.
Through open paths, our fates entwine,
In this vast world, where hearts align.

So let us wander, unafraid,
With love as compass, undismayed.
For in this life, so rich and fine,
We'll trace the stars, where hearts align.

Feelings' Geographic Secrets

In valleys deep, emotions grow,
Silent whispers softly flow.
Mountains high guard hidden cries,
Beneath the sun, the heart complies.

Rivers twist, a tale to tell,
Where laughter, love, and sorrow dwell.
Oceans wide, vast dreams they weave,
In every wave, we breathe, believe.

Soft winds carry hopes anew,
As clouds embrace the morning blue.
Each leaf rustles secrets wild,
A canvas bright, where hearts've compiled.

Canyons echo with lost desires,
Fires of passion, burning pyres.
A compass flawed, it leads us back,
To find our way along the track.

So map your heart, explore the land,
In every footprint, take a stand.
For in these depths, we learn to chart,
The winding paths of every heart.

The Current of Connection

A river flows between us two,
With every glance, a bond we grew.
Tides of trust pull gently near,
In quiet moments, hearts appear.

Like branches bending in the breeze,
We share a language, soft as leaves.
Each heartbeat echoes, a sweet refrain,
In this connection, joy and pain.

Bridges built from shared delight,
The current takes us through the night.
In laughter's light and sorrow's weight,
Our souls entwine, we navigate.

Through storms we stand, through calm we glide,
Two ships that sail with love as guide.
In every wave, we find our way,
The current strong, come what may.

So trust the flow, embrace the ride,
With open hearts, we shall abide.
For in these depths, we are set free,
Together bound, just you and me.

Turning Points

A shattered path beneath our feet,
With every step, the world repeats.
We pause in silence, breath held tight,
As shadows whisper through the night.

A compass spins, unsure the way,
Yet something calls us to stay.
In moments rare, choices arise,
Reflections dance in our own eyes.

From crossroads met with fear and doubt,
We gather strength to twist and shout.
The scars we bear, they shape our course,
In every heart, a hidden source.

And in the turning, futures spark,
A flame ignites within the dark.
With courage found, we leap ahead,
Embracing all that lies unsaid.

So here's to change, the unforeseen,
In every loss, a chance to glean.
In turning points, our spirits soar,
Discovering what life has in store.

Hearthstone Navigations

Amidst the warmth of flickering flame,
Home becomes a sacred name.
With hearthstone nestled, stories shared,
In every heartbeat, love is bared.

The scent of spice, the laughter spread,
In cozy corners, dreams are fed.
Each ember glows, a guiding light,
In shadowed hours, we'll hold on tight.

With every tale the night unfurls,
We weave our life in swirls and twirls.
Fireside chats and hopes expressed,
In every pause, our souls are blessed.

Through seasons change, our roots run deep,
In this warm glow, our secrets keep.
From dusk till dawn, we will abide,
Together on this warming tide.

So gather 'round, let stories flow,
In hearthstone's glow, our spirits grow.
For home is where the heart can rest,
In love's embrace, we are the best.

Secrets of the Journey

In the shadows where dreams unfold,
Stories hidden, yet to be told.
Every step whispers of the past,
Moments fleeting, but made to last.

Paths diverge under starlit skies,
Maps of the heart, where truth lies.
Each twist and turn, a lesson learned,
A flickering flame, brightly burned.

Gentle winds guide the soul's flight,
Through the dark and into the light.
Every secret holds a key,
Unlocking what is meant to be.

Time weaves tales with threads of gold,
In the silence, stories unfold.
Every journey a dance with fate,
In the tapestry of love, create.

Carry the whispers, embrace the call,
Secrets of the journey—share them all.
For every step, a tune to hum,
Together, we'll find where we're from.

Tides of Togetherness

Waves crash gently on sandy shores,
Ebbing and flowing, forevermore.
Hand in hand, we face the sea,
Tides whisper secrets, wild and free.

Moonlit nights guide our way,
Stars align in grand display.
With every rise, our spirits soar,
Unity's strength at the ocean's core.

In laughter shared, our hearts will swell,
In quiet moments, a soothing spell.
Like ocean currents, we drift and blend,
Bound by a love that will never end.

Seashells tell tales of where we've been,
In the depths, our souls glean.
Through storms that lash, we remain true,
Together we conquer, me and you.

As tides return to kiss the land,
We carve our dreams, hand in hand.
Forever dancing on this shore,
In the tides of love, we explore.

Whispers of Direction

In the quiet, a voice divine,
Guides us softly, intertwines.
Whispers of hope in the morning's light,
Pointing the way through darkest night.

Paths unfold with every breath,
Testing courage against fear's depth.
With each step, we're never alone,
Together we carve out what's our own.

Like leaves carried on the breeze,
We trust the whispers that aim to please.
They weave a map, so clear and bright,
Leading us home, into the light.

When doubts arise and shadows loom,
Listen close to the heart's sweet tune.
For every whisper is a spark,
Igniting paths within the dark.

In unison, let our voices soar,
Together we'll find what we're looking for.
In whispers soft, our truth reflects,
The direction love connects.

Navigating Love's Labyrinth

In a maze where hearts entwine,
Winding paths through whispers divine.
Every turn, a choice must be made,
In love's sweet game, we find our way.

Labyrinth echoes of laughter shared,
Moments cherished, love declared.
With hands entwined, we journey deep,
Through surprised corners, secrets keep.

Mistakes transform into lessons learned,
Within each knot, passion burned.
Mapping feelings with every gaze,
Navigating life through love's sweet haze.

As the walls shift, our hearts will grow,
Through tangled vines, our love will flow.
With every heartbeat that we trace,
In this labyrinth, we find our place.

So let's explore, my dear, together,
Every twist a dance, light as a feather.
In love's embrace, we shall reside,
Navigating joy, side by side.

The Horizon of Hope

Beyond the hills where sunlight gleams,
A promise whispers in soft beams.
With every dawn, we rise anew,
Chasing dreams that beckon true.

In fields of gold where shadows play,
We plant our hopes for a brighter day.
The skies may weep, yet hearts ignite,
For hope persists, our guiding light.

Through storms that rage and winds that howl,
We stand united, fierce and proud.
With every step, we dare to roam,
Together, we will find our home.

In silence deep, where truths unfold,
The horizon waits, a tale retold.
With courage bold, we face the sun,
In this vast world, we are not done.

So let us rise, hand in hand,
Together charting hope's vast land.
For every heart that beats with fire,
Is woven in this deep desire.

Rhythms of the Heart

In whispers soft, the heart begins,
A symphony where love transcends.
With every beat, a story told,
Of warmth and magic, brave and bold.

The dances sway like leaves in trees,
Carried on each gentle breeze.
In every glance, a silent call,
A melody that binds us all.

Time slips away in sweet embrace,
As rhythms set the world in place.
In laughter bright, our spirits soar,
A heartbeat echoes, wanting more.

Through joys and tears, we find our way,
In chords of love, we choose to stay.
A tapestry of moments shared,
In every note, our souls laid bare.

So let this rhythm guide our dance,
In every heartbeat, find romance.
Together, we create the art,
For life itself is a sacred heart.

The Signature of Affection

With ink of dreams, our hearts compose,
The signature of love that grows.
In letters soft where feelings flow,
Each curve and line, a tale we show.

In quiet moments, hands entwined,
We write the stories, hearts aligned.
With every word, a promise sealed,
In sacred bonds, our truths revealed.

Through trials faced and joys we've sought,
In every pause, the love we've caught.
Each moment penned with tender grace,
In every stroke, our shared embrace.

So let the pages turn anew,
As life unfolds in shades of blue.
In every chapter, love's refrain,
In every line, its sweet refrain.

Together we will write our tale,
In whispers soft, we shall not fail.
For in our hearts, the ink still flows,
The signature of love that glows.

Paths of Connection

In winding roads where footsteps meet,
The threads of life weave tales so sweet.
Through every turn and twist we find,
The paths that link our hearts and minds.

Through tangled roots and open skies,
We discover truth behind the lies.
With every step, we share the light,
In every heart, a spark ignites.

With open arms and kindness shared,
We journey forth, our love declared.
In bridges built, we find our way,
Across the dark, towards the day.

Together we face the storms that come,
In unity, we find our home.
Through valleys low and mountains high,
Connection's thread will never die.

So let us walk these paths in trust,
In every choice, in love we must.
For journeys shared are never lost,
In every step, we pay the cost.

Love's Guiding Light

In twilight's soft embrace we stand,
With dreams ablaze like grains of sand.
Your laughter dances in the air,
A melody that banishes despair.

Through shadows deep, we find our way,
Each whispered word, a promise to stay.
Our hearts entwined, a radiant spark,
You are my fire, lighting the dark.

With every step, love's journey flows,
A river deep where passion grows.
Through all the storms, we sail as one,
Guided by light, until the day is done.

Together we rise, together we fall,
In this sacred dance, we hear the call.
Hand in hand, forever we'll roam,
In love's embrace, we are home.

So let the stars our path ignite,
In the embrace of love's guiding light.
With every heartbeat, in joy we soar,
Forevermore, forevermore.

The Compass Rose of Emotion

In the map of life, emotions reside,
A compass rose where hearts abide.
Each direction sings a different tune,
Guiding lost souls beneath the moon.

With north winds true, I follow your call,
Through tempest and calm, we rise, we fall.
South brings warmth, in gentle embrace,
Your love a haven, my sacred space.

East holds the dawn, with hope anew,
While west whispers dreams, and skies so blue.
In every breath, your essence I trace,
A journey of hearts in this endless space.

Together we navigate uncharted seas,
With faith and trust, carried by the breeze.
The compass spins, yet we remain near,
Guided by love, erasing all fear.

In the dance of life, let us explore,
The compass rose, forevermore.
With passionate hearts, our spirits collide,
In this great adventure, we're side by side.

Vistas of Yearning

On the horizon, dreams softly gleam,
Vistas of yearning, an endless dream.
With each sunrise, a new hope unfolds,
A canvas of stories waiting to be told.

In valleys deep, under skies so wide,
Our hearts paint pictures where love can reside.
With every glance, the world spins bright,
Illuminated paths, leading to the light.

Through forests dense, where silence sings,
The whispers of love, on delicate wings.
Every heartbeat echoes, a soft refrain,
In the depth of longing, a sweet, sweet pain.

Atop the mountains, we stand so tall,
Knowing in unity, we can conquer all.
With arms wide open, we embrace the day,
In vistas of yearning, forever we'll stay.

So let the winds carry our dream afar,
In the tapestry of life, you are my star.
Together we'll wander, together we'll find,
The vistas of longing, two hearts aligned.

The Intersection of Hearts

In the crossroads of fate, we find our way,
Two souls converging, come what may.
With every glance, a spark ignites,
In the intersection, our love delights.

Here in the stillness, time stands still,
As whispered secrets begin to spill.
With fingers entwined, we take a chance,
In this dance of love, a timeless romance.

In the laughter shared, and the tears we shed,
The intersection grows, where angels tread.
With each moment lived, our spirits soar,
In the embrace of love, forevermore.

Through paths unknown, we boldly stride,
With hearts wide open, let love be our guide.
In the tapestry woven, we create our part,
A masterpiece born from the intersection of hearts.

So take my hand, let's journey far,
In the light of love, where we are.
With every heartbeat, let the world see,
In the intersection of hearts, you and me.

Guiding Emotions

In shadows deep, we find our way,
A compass of the heart each day.
Emotions rise like waves on shore,
We steer through storms, we seek for more.

In laughter's light, we breathe anew,
Through tears we learn what love can do.
Each moment shapes our tender ties,
Our hearts will speak, our spirits rise.

With whispers soft, we chart our course,
In every glance, a hidden source.
Through trials faced, we grow and bend,
Together, we will always mend.

The hues of passion paint our skies,
In every challenge, love replies.
Through autumn's chill and summer's heat,
We dance in rhythm, hearts will beat.

As guiding stars above us gleam,
We find our path, we chase the dream.
With every step, we're not alone,
In guiding emotions, love has grown.

Navigating Love's Tide

In the ocean of feelings, we drift and glide,
Navigating the currents, with you by my side.
The waves may crash, the winds may roar,
But our love is a harbor, a safe distant shore.

With each ebb and flow, our hearts align,
In the dance of the sea, your hand in mine.
Together we sail through tempest and calm,
Your laughter echoes, a soothing balm.

When storms arise, and shadows loom,
We anchor our hopes in the softest bloom.
For love is a compass, guiding our way,
Through the darkest nights and brightest days.

With the stars above and the moon's soft glow,
We chart our destiny, love's gentle flow.
In whispers of dreams, we find our place,
Navigating love's tide, in warm embrace.

As seasons change and the tides will shift,
In every heartbeat, our spirits lift.
Together, we journey, fearless and free,
In the ocean of love, you and me.

Whispers of the Soul

In silence deep, where thoughts reside,
Whispers of the soul, a gentle guide.
Echoes of dreams, in twilight's hue,
We listen close to what feels true.

With every heartbeat, secrets unfold,
The stories of longing, timeless and bold.
In soft reflections, shadows embrace,
Each moment a treasure, an endless space.

Through eyes that meet, a language shared,
A symphony of souls, profoundly bared.
In the warmth of the gaze, the world ignites,
Whispers of love in endless nights.

With every sigh, the spirit soars,
In the dance of the heart, it opens doors.
Together we weave, in harmony's flow,
Whispers of the soul, forever aglow.

As time slips by, in tender grace,
We cherish the moments our souls embrace.
In the stillness of night, as dreams unfold,
Whispers of the soul, a story retold.

Directions of Desire

In the labyrinth of longing, we find our way,
Directions of desire, come what may.
With every heartbeat, the flame ignites,
A fire within, that gently invites.

In the realm of passion, we intertwine,
Two souls united, our fates aligned.
Like stars that shimmer in the velvet sky,
With each tender touch, we learn to fly.

In whispers soft, our dreams take flight,
Navigating desires, through day and night.
With courage to chase what the heart demands,
Together we stand, hand in hand.

Through valleys low and mountains high,
In the quest for love, we reach for the sky.
For every longing, there's beauty to find,
Directions of desire, both heart and mind.

As time unwinds, we'll never tire,
For love is a journey, the greatest desire.
Through every challenge, we'll find our way,
In the directions of desire, forever we'll stay.

Pathways of Passion

In twilight's glow, dreams ignite,
Whispers of love take flight.
Through winding roads, hearts explore,
Eager footsteps, yearning for more.

Each turn reveals a hidden glance,
Where souls entwine, a fleeting chance.
The fire within, a guiding light,
Burning brightly through the night.

With every laugh, every sigh,
Moments cherished as time goes by.
In the dance of fate, we twirl,
Passion's embrace, a wondrous swirl.

Together we forge an endless way,
In the warmth of love's ballet.
From dusk to dawn, hearts will chase,
In these pathways, we find our place.

So let us wander, hand in hand,
Through fields of dreams, across the land.
With each heartbeat, a story spins,
In pathways of passion, our life begins.

The Compass of Solitude

In silence deep, the shadows weave,
A compass guides, I dare believe.
Lonely paths where thoughts reside,
In the stillness, I confide.

With every breath, the world retreats,
Echoes of the heart, soft beats.
In solitude, I find my way,
Searching for the light of day.

Moments drift like autumn leaves,
Wanderlust in the heart believes.
Through the echoes of my mind,
In quietude, truths I find.

The compass spins, a gentle dance,
Every shadow holds a chance.
Navigating through the vast unknown,
In solitude, I stand alone.

Yet in the hush, I find my song,
A melody where I belong.
Each note a step, a brand new start,
The compass leads me to my heart.

Between Beats and Dreams

In the stillness, pulses thrum,
A rhythm calls, my thoughts succumb.
Between each beat, a vision glows,
In fragile realms, the dreamer flows.

The sun dips low, horizons swirl,
In twilight's breath, our secrets unfurl.
Every heartbeat, a promise made,
In shadows of night, where dreams invade.

As starlight weaves through velvet skies,
I chase the glimmers in your eyes.
Bound by whispers, hopes align,
Between beats and dreams, we intertwine.

With every sigh, the world expands,
In your embrace, eternity stands.
Together we dance, lost in time,
Between beats and dreams, our lives rhyme.

So let us soar, on wings of fate,
In this space where we create.
Forever bound by love's sweet seam,
In the silence between beats and dreams.

The Cartographer of Desire

With ink-stained hands, I trace the lines,
Mapping out each heart's designs.
The contours of longing, valleys deep,
In the terrain, secrets we keep.

A compass spins with every glance,
In the map of love, we take a chance.
Uncharted paths through vibrant lands,
Fingers entwined like golden strands.

Through mountains high and rivers wide,
In the landscapes where dreams confide.
Every touch, a legend born,
In the heart's atlas, love is adorned.

The cartographer draws with fervent art,
Sketching the place where echoes start.
In a world unknown, desire's flame,
Illuminates the heart's true name.

So let us wander, map in hand,
Discover jewels in love's vast land.
Together we sketch through endless skies,
As the cartographer of desire, our passion flies.

The Adventure of Belonging

In a land where whispers roam,
Hearts find paths, a place called home.
Together we dance under the stars,
Each step a story, no more scars.

Through laughter shared, and dreams so bright,
We build a refuge, warm and light.
In every glance, a silent vow,
This is our moment, this is our now.

Through trials faced, we stand as one,
Chasing horizons, beneath the sun.
With every heartbeat, the bond grows strong,
In the adventure of belonging, we all belong.

United by each joy and fear,
In the tapestry of life, we draw near.
With open arms, we welcome fate,
An adventure awaits, together we create.

So here's to the journey, hand in hand,
In the adventure of belonging, we take a stand.
With every moment that life brings,
Together we soar on love's sweet wings.

The Sounding of Emotion

In the quiet chambers of the heart,
Echoes of feelings, each a sacred art.
A gentle sigh, a heartfelt plea,
In the sounding of emotion, we find the key.

With every tear that falls like rain,
We unveil love, we confront the pain.
A symphony played on strings of soul,
In the music of feelings, we become whole.

Joy dances lightly, sorrow holds tight,
In the rhythm of life, day turns to night.
In each heartbeat, in every tune,
The sounding of emotion, beneath the moon.

We share our laughter, share our cries,
Together we soar, we learn to rise.
In the depths of sentiment, we find our place,
In the sounding of emotion, we embrace grace.

So let the melody resonate and flow,
In the orchestra of feelings, let love glow.
With each note played, let the truth ignite,
In the sounding of emotion, there's pure light.

Anchored in Affection

In the stormy seas of doubt and fear,
Love stands firm, ever near.
With every wave that crashes down,
We find our strength, never to drown.

Holding fast through darkest nights,
In the glow of stars, we find our sights.
Roots entwined in the soil deep,
Anchored in affection, promises we keep.

Through whispers soft and gestures warm,
We weather the chaos, embrace the storm.
With hands entwined, we brave the quest,
Anchored in affection, we are truly blessed.

With every heartbeat, our love expands,
In the fabric of time, we weave our strands.
Together we rise, together we stand,
Anchored in affection, hand in hand.

So let the tides of life come and go,
In the depth of love, we endlessly grow.
In every challenge, we find our way,
Anchored in affection, forever we stay.

The Threads of Connection

In the woven fabric of every day,
Threads of connection gently lay.
In laughter shared and stories told,
We find the warmth amidst the cold.

In every smile, a bond is spun,
A tapestry formed, two hearts as one.
Through whispered dreams, we intertwine,
The threads of connection, divine design.

Through seasons' change, we learn to adapt,
In the dance of life, we're all entrapped.
With each connection, a spark ignites,
The threads of connection light up the nights.

With patience woven, and kindness sown,
In each encounter, we've brightly grown.
In the gentle pull of hands that meet,
The threads of connection feel so sweet.

So let the fabric ever expand,
In the threads of connection, let love stand.
Through every layer, the truth we find,
We're intricately woven, hearts entwined.

Undulating Currents of Affection

Waves whisper soft on the shore,
Hearts entwined, craving more.
Beneath the moon's gentle sway,
Love flows deeply, night and day.

Tides rise and grant us flight,
Stars shimmer, guiding light.
In each caress, we find our way,
Undulating, come what may.

Through storms and currents that shift,
Together, we are the gift.
In every rise, in every fall,
Our love, the anchor through it all.

Echoes of laughter dance in the breeze,
Time slows down, our hearts at ease.
With every crest, we learn, we grow,
A sea of feelings, ever in flow.

Let the waves in whispers resound,
In this current, our souls are found.
With every tide, we sail and trust,
In love's embrace, it's always a must.

A Love Without Borders

Across the mountains, wide and grand,
Our hearts unite, hand in hand.
From desert sands to oceans blue,
A love that knows no bounds, just grew.

Through every land, our journey's sweet,
Together, we face each heartbeat.
No distance can our love betray,
In dreams, we meet, come what may.

The stars above mark our endless quest,
In every whisper, we find our rest.
With laughter echoing through the years,
We conquer doubts and shed our fears.

A bond that stretches, not confined,
In every heartbeat, you are my mind.
Together, we roam each foreign street,
In laughter and love, our souls complete.

With every mile, our spirits soar,
In every moment, we want more.
A love that dances through skies and seas,
Without borders, just you and me.

The Scenic Route of Romance

Winding paths beneath the trees,
Hand in hand, with gentle ease.
Every turn reveals a new view,
In love's embrace, just me and you.

Sunset paints the skies in gold,
Whispered dreams start to unfold.
Through valleys deep and hills so high,
Together we bask, just you and I.

The quiet moments, soft and sweet,
Where heartbeats sing and softly meet.
With laughter echoing in the air,
We savor each moment, truly rare.

Each detour offers joy unknown,
In every step, our love has grown.
As stars emerge, a guiding light,
On this scenic route, hearts take flight.

Let's wander where the wildflowers bloom,
In every breath, dispel the gloom.
Through nature's beauty, we find our way,
Together forever, come what may.

Cartography of the Soul

Maps unfold in silent grace,
Tracing lines, we find our place.
In every curve, in every sprawl,
We paint the love that conquers all.

With compass hearts, we chart the skies,
Navigating with trusting eyes.
Through mountains high and valleys wide,
Together, we are side by side.

The journey etched on every page,
Writing stories free from cage.
In ink of heart, our dreams unfurl,
A tapestry of a boundless world.

Every moment, a point in time,
Together we create our rhyme.
In whispers soft, our map takes shape,
A love that time cannot escape.

So let's explore with open hearts,
In every twist, fresh love imparts.
Through paths unknown, let's always roam,
In the map of us, we find our home.

Mapping Intuition's Path

In whispers soft, the road unfurls,
A guide unseen in hidden swirls.
With every step, the heart will sway,
As shadows dance, and light will play.

Maps scribbled on the edge of night,
Where instincts call, and fears take flight.
Each twist and turn, a chance to weave,
The tapestry of what we believe.

Through brambles thick and mountains steep,
Intuition speaks, the secrets keep.
Within the silence, truth will bloom,
Casting out the lingering gloom.

In every pause, a choice will rise,
A compass drawn beneath the skies.
With faith as fuel, the journey's light,
We dare to dream, to take the flight.

So heed the signs, let passions flow,
For intuition knows the way to go.
In every heart, a map resides,
An endless path where hope abides.

Stars Above

In the velvet sky, they shimmer bright,
Whispers of dreams in the cloak of night.
Each twinkle tells a story old,
Of wishes cast and hearts so bold.

They guide the sailors on the sea,
A tapestry woven, wild and free.
In cosmic dance, they swirl and glow,
A reminder of paths we long to know.

Some say they hold the past's embrace,
Memories scattered in time and space.
While others see the future's face,
In every star, a hidden place.

The moon hangs low, a watchful friend,
As night unfolds, we start to mend.
With every glance, we trace the lines,
Connecting hearts where fate entwines.

So lift your gaze, let wonder reign,
In starry depths, we find our gain.
For in their light, we see the true,
The dreams that spark and bring us through.

Feelings Below

In the depths of silence, whispers grow,
Beneath the surface, tides ebb and flow.
Emotions buried, soft as clay,
Yearn to rise and greet the day.

The heartbeats echo, deep and strong,
In shadows hidden, where they belong.
Each pulse a tale of love and fear,
A symphony only few can hear.

Memories linger, like ghostly scents,
Haunting the dreams where time condense.
Each moment counts, a fleeting grace,
In the quiet depths, we find our place.

So dive inside, embrace the wave,
For feelings below are what we crave.
With every surge, a truth unspun,
In the vastness, we become one.

From depths so dark, a light shall glean,
A luminous path, a vibrant sheen.
Feelings below, a treasure rare,
Unlock the soul, if hearts dare.

The Cartographer of Dreams

With ink and quill, the maps are drawn,
Of realms where daylight meets the dawn.
Each winding line, a path unclear,
Yet beckons forth, inviting fear.

Through valleys deep and mountains high,
The dreams unfold, like clouds in the sky.
A world unseen, rich with desire,
Where hopes ignite and hearts conspire.

With every stroke, a journey starts,
Navigating through the shifting arts.
In twilight hues, adventures blend,
The map of dreams that shall not end.

The stars emerge, the compass spins,
Guiding us where the magic begins.
In the cartographer's steady hand,
Are stories waiting to be planned.

So carve your path, let visions guide,
With courage strong and arms spread wide.
For in the dreams, real maps reside,
A universe where souls collide.

Pulse of the Journey

In every heartbeat, stories dwell,
Rhythms echo, a haunting swell.
Each step we take, a dance of chance,
A tapestry woven in life's romance.

The mountains call, the rivers flow,
Each pulse a signal, an inner glow.
With every mile, the spirit sings,
The pulse of life, the joy it brings.

Through storms that rage and skies so clear,
The journey's truth, we hold so dear.
In laughter shared and tears we cry,
The pulse of the journey lifts us high.

With every turn, the lessons learned,
In fires of passion, the heart has burned.
So let your feet tread paths unknown,
For in each pulse, you'll find your home.

So chase the dawn, embrace the night,
With every heartbeat, journey right.
For life's a poem, a vibrant spree,
The pulse of the journey, wild and free.

Tides of Commitment

On the shore where waves collide,
Promises made, side by side.
Under the sun's warm embrace,
Hearts entwined in a sacred space.

Through the storms that come our way,
Together we'll stand, come what may.
Each tide a testament strong,
In the rhythm where we belong.

Hand in hand on this shifting sand,
Our love the anchor, forever we'll stand.
With each surge, our vows renew,
In the ocean of me and you.

As the moon pulls the sea,
So do you pull me closer, you see.
In the depths of our devotion,
We've crafted a love's unending potion.

With every swell and every retreat,
Our bond grows stronger, bittersweet.
In the tides of commitment, we trust,
For love is eternal, it's a must.

Celestial Coordinates of Love

Under a sky where stars align,
We chart a course, your hand in mine.
Galaxies weave their ancient lore,
Mapping the love we both adore.

Every heartbeat a cosmic sign,
In this vast universe, you are divine.
Through the night, you light my way,
Guiding me near, come what may.

Constellations whisper our fate,
In the alignment, we resonate.
From distant moons to the sun's bright glow,
Together we journey, forever we'll flow.

As satellites dance in synchronized flight,
Our souls entwined in love's pure light.
From meteors to comets, we'll soar,
Navigating love's open door.

With every pulse echoing through space,
I find my home in your embrace.
In this celestial embrace, we're free,
Forever bound, just you and me.

The Orbits of Affection

In the dance of our orbiting hearts,
Each revolution, a brand new start.
With every shift, feelings abound,
In the gravity of love, we are found.

Round and round, like planets we spin,
In this cosmos, where love begins.
Through the ages, our path intertwines,
Charting the course of love's designs.

With the sun's warmth, our spirits ignite,
Navigating together, in day and in night.
As comets streak across the skies,
So too does our love, ever wise.

Gravity holds us in its embrace,
In this vast universe, we find our place.
Eclipsing doubts with passionate kin,
In the orbital dance, we both win.

Across galaxies, through time and space,
Our affection transcends, leaving a trace.
Embracing the cycles, hand in hand,
In the orbits of love, forever we stand.

Routes of Remembrance

In the paths we walk, memories bloom,
Guided by whispers in quiet rooms.
Each step we take, echoes of grace,
Tracing the lines of our shared space.

Moments cherished like precious gold,
Stories of love, steadfast and bold.
In the shadows of time, we find the light,
Routes of remembrance, hearts shining bright.

With every turn and winding lane,
We gather the joy, even the pain.
In laughter and tears, we find what's real,
The routes of the past, forever we feel.

Through the years, our journey unfolds,
Tales of adventure in whispers told.
As footprints linger on familiar ground,
In the dance of remembering, love is found.

So here's to the trails that brought us here,
In the tapestry woven, your voice I hear.
With each route taken, our spirits soar,
In the routes of remembrance, I love you more.

Fables of Intuition

In whispers soft, the truth reveals,
A tale of heart, it gently heals.
The flicker of a thought, so bright,
Guides us through shadows, towards the light.

Like leaves that dance on summer's breeze,
Intuition flows, as calm as seas.
Each moment counts, a subtle guide,
In silent echoes, we must confide.

Embrace the signs that life bestows,
For in their grasp, the wisdom grows.
Within the stillness, answers speak,
The heart's soft voice is never weak.

Trust the compass that lies within,
It knows the path where dreams begin.
With open minds, we shall explore,
The fables whispered forevermore.

The Path to Togetherness

In every step, a bond refined,
The road we share, two hearts aligned.
Through laughter's glow and sorrows shared,
A tapestry of love, we've dared.

With hands entwined, we face the storm,
In unity, we find our form.
The trials faced, a journey long,
But in our hearts, we stay so strong.

Each whispered word, a sacred trust,
We build our dreams, as all must.
In moments small, our love's embrace,
Together we shall find our place.

As sunsets paint the evening sky,
Our hopes take flight, forever high.
With every dawn, a promise true,
On this path, it's me and you.

Navigating Through Dreams

In slumber's reach, our spirits soar,
To worlds unseen, we long for more.
Like ships at sea, we glide on night,
Through twilight's charm, we seek the light.

Each dream a key, a map we hold,
Unlocking secrets, brave and bold.
With every thought, the stars align,
In realms of wonder, all is divine.

As shadows wane, new visions bloom,
The heart's delight, dispelling gloom.
In whispered dreams, we find our way,
To brighter paths, we shall not stray.

With open hearts, we chase the dawn,
For in our dreams, we are reborn.
With every breath, let courage gleam,
Together we will chase the dream.

The Compass of Destiny

In every choice, the threads weave tight,
A tapestry of day and night.
With every turn, the path unfolds,
As destiny's hand in silence holds.

Through winding roads and trials faced,
Our journey's drawn, our fears embraced.
The compass points, forever true,
Towards dreams that wait, both old and new.

In moments still, we hear the call,
To rise above, to never fall.
With courage as our guiding star,
We navigate, no matter how far.

Embrace the winds, let spirits soar,
For in each heartbeat lies the lore.
The compass spins, yet stays aligned,
As we discover what's truly ours to find.

Uncharted Territories of the Soul

In depths where silence dwells,
We wander lost and free.
Through shadows we hear whispers,
Of dreams yet to decree.

Each step unveils new wonders,
A landscape unrefined.
With courage, we discover,
The treasures of the mind.

The heart, a compass guiding,
Amidst the unknown seas.
Past mountains of our stories,
We find our destinies.

Through valleys rich with longing,
And rivers of pure thought.
We chart the unseen heavens,
In threads of love we've sought.

In this vast expanse we gather,
The pieces of our whole.
Unraveling our edges,
We claim our sacred role.

Love's Latitude and Longitude

A map drawn tenderly,
Where hearts find their true place.
Each point a whispered promise,
In love's eternal grace.

The distance we traverse,
In shadows and in light.
Coordinates of our laughter,
And tears we've learned to fight.

With every degree measured,
We find what we should hold.
A journey marked by starlight,
And stories yet untold.

In valleys of sweet longing,
Together we align.
Through storms and sunny skies,
Our hearts in sync, divine.

At this junction of our lives,
We forge our way ahead.
With love's vast expanse before us,
In faith, we're surely led.

The Journey of the Unspoken

In silence blooms a longing,
A voice that dares not speak.
Unfolding through our gazes,
In every glance we seek.

The weight of all we cherish,
Remains beneath the skin.
As echoes bridge the distance,
A symphony within.

Each moment shared in silence,
A world below the sound.
The uncharted depths of feelings,
Where connection can be found.

Through shadows of our stories,
We navigate the night.
In whispers of the heart,
We draw our dreams to light.

So here we stand together,
Embracing what's unseen.
The journey of the unspoken,
In love, a silent dream.

Terrain of Tenderness

A sanctuary of softness,
Where hearts can gently sway.
The ground beneath us trembles,
In love's familiar way.

With every breath we take,
We cultivate the space.
In gardens rich with silence,
We plant our warm embrace.

Through paths of understanding,
We wander hand in hand.
In valleys deep with kindness,
We learn to understand.

The mountains high with patience,
Stand witness to our truth.
In every hill we climb,
Resides the power of youth.

This terrain of tenderness,
A treasure we explore.
Together in this journey,
We'll always seek for more.

Giggles in the Breeze

Laughter dances through the trees,
Carried softly by the breeze.
Whispers of joy, the world alight,
Children's smiles, pure and bright.

Butterflies flutter, a playful game,
Every child, a heart untamed.
Chasing shadows, spinning around,
In nature's playground, joy is found.

Clouds drift lazily high above,
Embracing life, like rays of love.
Each giggle echoes, sweet and clear,
In the warm embrace of summer near.

Gentle winds weave through the day,
As laughter guides us on our way.
With every sigh, the world's a song,
In this moment, we all belong.

Together we weave memories anew,
In the breeze, a magic view.
A tapestry of joy unwinds,
As giggles linger in our minds.

Sketches of Romance

Underneath the moonlit sky,
Two hearts whisper, shy and nigh.
Softened glances, a lingering touch,
In this silence, they speak so much.

Canvas of dreams painted bright,
Every stroke feels just right.
With every heartbeat, passion grows,
In quiet moments, true love shows.

Hands entwined, their fingers trace,
A delicate dance, a timeless grace.
Sweet serenades linger in air,
With every glance, a promise shared.

Gentle laughter fills the night,
Creating memories, pure delight.
In this story, they're both the art,
Sketches of love, two beating hearts.

Through life's canvas, side by side,
A love so deep, it cannot hide.
Each moment crafted, a cherished view,
In sketches of romance, forever true.

Allure of the Unknown

In shadows cast by moonlit glow,
The mysteries call from below.
Paths unworn, secrets await,
With each step, we tempt fate.

Eager hearts and open minds,
Adventure whispers, truth unwinds.
The thrill of the chase, the fear of the dark,
Igniting the spark, a wandering heart.

Stars above, a guiding light,
Leading us on through the deep night.
With every turn, a chance to grow,
In the allure of the unknown.

Hope unfolds, like a flower rare,
In the face of fears, we learn to dare.
Each story unfolds, waiting for sign,
In uncharted lands, the stars align.

Together we'll journey, hand in hand,
Through twists and turns in this vast land.
With courage ignited, we'll face the flow,
Embracing the wonder, the unknown we sow.

Recipes of the Heart

A pinch of joy, a dash of grace,
Mix together, time and space.
Measure love, warmth so sweet,
Stir it gently, life's a treat.

Sprinkle laughter, an endless supply,
Top it with dreams that love can't deny.
Bake with patience, let it rise,
In the warmth of love, the soul flies.

Simmer kindness, never let it go,
In every bite, let affection flow.
Whisk away worries, add a cheer,
In every moment, keep loved ones near.

Garnished with hope, serve it warm,
In the kitchen, love's the norm.
Each recipe shared, a heart's embrace,
Cooking together, time slows its pace.

So gather around, let stories start,
For life's best flavors are recipes of the heart.
In this dish, we find our way,
Creating memories day by day.

Emotional Bearings

In shadows deep, we seek the light,
Whispers calm the raging night.
Hearts collide in silent screams,
Finding solace in our dreams.

Paths unfold like tender leaves,
Holding on to what we believe.
Embers glow through trials faced,
In the warmth, our fears are traced.

With every tear, a story grows,
In every laugh, the spirit flows.
Finding strength in woven ties,
This journey blurs the sunset skies.

Time stands still in moments shared,
In love's embrace, we are repaired.
Each heartbeat sings a gentle tune,
Guiding us like the silver moon.

Together we rise, unyielding sands,
Holding tight with hopeful hands.
Every step, a dance of fate,
In unity, we celebrate.

The Navigational Rhythm

Across the sea, the stars align,
With every wave, your heart is mine.
Charting courses through the storm,
In our embrace, the world feels warm.

A compass set by love's strong hand,
Guides us through this endless sand.
In every beat, a promise flows,
Together as the moonlight glows.

The tides may turn, but we won't sway,
Anchored firm in love's array.
In every ebb, there's bliss to find,
A navigational rhythm, intertwined.

With sails unfurled, the wind will sing,
In harmony, our spirits take wing.
Voyagers on this vast expanse,
Finding joy in every chance.

So let the stars their secrets tell,
In every heartbeat, we'll dwell.
Through storms and calms, we'll always chart,
The navigational rhythm of the heart.

Heartstrings and Horizons

Strings of fate pull gently tight,
Beneath the vast, embracing night.
With every tug, our souls entwine,
Creating music, pure and fine.

Horizon stretches, far and wide,
Where dreams and hopes dare to reside.
In colors bright, we find our place,
In heartstrings' dance, we leave our trace.

The melodies of laughter play,
Woven in the words we say.
Every note, a tale of grace,
Resonating in time and space.

As morning breaks and shadows flee,
In unity, we claim the sea.
Together, we embrace the dawn,
With heartstrings tied, forever drawn.

So let us roam where skies touch earth,
In every moment, find rebirth.
Heartstrings and horizons, perfectly spun,
In every heartbeat, we are one.

The Drift of Belonging

In gentle waves, we float along,
To shores where our hearts feel strong.
Each whisper wraps us like a shawl,
In the drift, we find our all.

The tides may pull, the winds may shift,
In every moment, love's sweet gift.
As seasons change, our roots run deep,
In this embrace, our promises keep.

Memories weave a tapestry bright,
Guiding us through the darkest night.
In laughter shared and burdens lifted,
Our hearts entwined, forever gifted.

So here we are, in this expanse,
With open hearts, we take the chance.
Together we rise, in light we bask,
In the drift of belonging, we unmask.

For in this journey, we are free,
To be ourselves, just you and me.
In quiet moments, we belong,
A symphony, a whispered song.

Inward Voyage

In silence deep, the shadows dwell,
A journey starts, we know so well.
Beneath the waves, our thoughts do swim,
Into the heart's dark, brimming brim.

With every breath, the stillness grows,
A whispered truth, the spirit knows.
Through winding paths, our dreams take flight,
In quiet depths, we find the light.

The currents pull, with gentle might,
Each wave a thought, both dark and bright.
In search of solace, we dive deeper,
Embracing all, the wise and seeker.

Moments flow, like rivers run,
In the silence, we've just begun.
Unravel threads of fear and doubt,
Inward voyage, let love shout.

To every heartbeat, a new refrain,
The joys and sorrows, all the pain.
As we emerge from this sacred quest,
Inward voyage, we find our rest.

Uncharted Affections

In secret glances, feelings bloom,
A subtle dance, dispelling gloom.
With every smile, a story shared,
In uncharted lands, hearts laid bare.

Whispers soft, in twilight's glow,
A tender touch, the sparks do flow.
In shadows cast, love's map is drawn,
Through winding paths, we journey on.

Emotions swell, like tides at sea,
In unexplored realms, we dare to be.
With every pulse, a new emotion,
Uncharted affections, deep as ocean.

Through open fields, our laughter flies,
In gentle breezes, love replies.
With every moment, life ignites,
In uncharted dreams, we find our sights.

A canvas vast, we paint with grace,
Creating worlds in our embrace.
With love as guide, we'll never part,
Uncharted affections, two beating hearts.

The North Star of Passion

In the silence, a beacon bright,
A guiding force, our hearts take flight.
With every dream, it leads the way,
The North Star shines, come what may.

Through storms that rage, through nights so long,
In its glow, we find our song.
With every hope, its light ignites,
The North Star gleams on restless nights.

Paths unknown, under skies so vast,
With passion's flame, we hold it fast.
In swirling doubts, it burns so clear,
The North Star whispers, 'I am near.'

No matter the distance, nor shadow cast,
The fire within will ever last.
In heart's embrace, we soar above,
The North Star guides us, fueled by love.

So here we stand, united and strong,
In the embrace where we belong.
Forever drawn, like moth to flame,
The North Star of passion calls our name.

Echoes on the Wind

In quiet whispers, secrets roam,
Echoes carried far from home.
With every breeze, a tale unfolds,
In gentle tones, the heart consoles.

Through fields of dreams, the murmurs play,
In rustling leaves, they find their way.
Each sigh and laugh, a memory spun,
Echoes on the wind, a love begun.

From distant shores, the voices call,
In harmony, we rise and fall.
With every gust, we learn to fly,
Echoes blend with the evening sky.

In twilight's glow, the shadows dance,
A fleeting moment, a timeless chance.
Together woven, our spirits sing,
Echoes on the wind, forever cling.

In every corner, in every heart,
The echoes linger, never apart.
Through night and day, through storm and calm,
Echoes on the wind, a soothing balm.

Charting the Unseen

In shadows deep, we map the stars,
Whispers of dreams, both near and far.
Paths unwritten, in silence they dwell,
Secrets of time, in stories we tell.

Across the waves, the moon's soft glow,
Guiding hearts where wild winds blow.
Each compass point, a heart's true call,
In the vast unknown, we rise, we fall.

With every step, the unknown reveals,
Waves of fate, the heart it steals.
Through fog and mist, we carve our way,
To touch the dawn, a brand new day.

Through valleys low and mountains high,
We chase the dreams that never die.
In every heartbeat, we find our place,
A journey of love, an endless grace.

So chart the stars, embrace the night,
In unseen paths lies hidden light.
For in the dark, we learn to see,
The beauty of what's meant to be.

North of Nostalgia

In the attic of time, memories spin,
Echoes of laughter, where to begin?
Winter's embrace, a familiar song,
North of nostalgia, where we belong.

Footsteps on streets that whisper our name,
Flickers of youth, burning like flame.
Photographs faded, but feelings stay bright,
In the corners of heart, a soft, golden light.

Seasons change, yet love remains,
Heartfelt moments, like gentle rains.
Under the stars, we share our dreams,
In the fabric of time, nothing is as it seems.

Through windows of time, we gaze and sigh,
The warmth of the past, like a lullaby.
Every heartbeat echoes a tune,
In the north of nostalgia, we find our ruin.

So let us wander, hand in hand,
Back to the places we once did stand.
Memories linger, a heartfelt embrace,
In the tapestry of time, we carve our space.

The Unfolding Atlas

Pages of dreams in hand, we trace,
An atlas of hopes, our firm embrace.
Each line a journey, each fold a key,
Unlocking the wonders of what could be.

Mountains that rise like whispers of fate,
Oceans that pulse, hearts vibrate.
In the stretch of the map, horizons expand,
A canvas of lives, drawn by our hand.

With every turn, new stories unfold,
Treasures of life, both timid and bold.
Through valleys of doubt and peaks of delight,
We navigate stars, we soar to new heights.

The compass within guides us through night,
A promise of dawn, a future so bright.
In the unfolding atlas, we find our place,
In the vastness of life, we embrace our grace.

So let us journey, forever we seek,
The tales of the heart, the wisdom we speak.
In every page turned, a new chance to start,
The unfolding atlas, our work of art.

Signals in the Silence

In quiet moments, whispers collide,
Signals emerge where shadows hide.
A breath of hope, a glance from afar,
In the stillness, we find who we are.

Under the surface, the echoes resound,
Tales of the heart that can't be unbound.
In absent words, we weave our song,
The silence speaks, where we belong.

Through veils of quiet, connections ignite,
A dance of souls in the soft twilight.
With every heartbeat, a truth unveils,
In the space between, our love prevails.

Calling through darkness, the dreamers awake,
Bridges of light, every step we take.
In the hush of the world, we hear the call,
Signals in silence, connecting us all.

So let us linger in this sacred space,
Embrace the stillness, the gentle grace.
For in the quiet, we truly find,
The signals of love that unite humankind.